HORSEPOWER

RALLY CARS

by Carrie A. Braulick

Reading Consultant:
Barbara J. Fox
Reading Specialist
North Carolina State University

Content Consultant:
Pego Mack, Rally Manager
Sports Car Club of America
Topeka, Kansas

Capstone
press

Mankato, Minnesota

Blazers is published by Capstone Press,
151 Good Counsel Drive, P.O. Box 669, Mankato, Minnesota 56002.
www.capstonepress.com

Library of Congress Cataloging-in-Publication Data
Braulick, Carrie A., 1975–
Rally cars / by Carrie A. Braulick.
   p. cm.—(Blazers. Horsepower)
   Summary: "Describes rally cars, their main features, and how
they are raced"—Provided by publisher.
   Includes bibliographical references and index.
   ISBN–13: 978-0-7368-6784-9 (hardcover)
   ISBN–10: 0-7368-6784-8 (hardcover)
   1. Automobiles, Racing—Juvenile literature. 2. Automobile rallys—Juvenile
literature. I. Title. II. Series.
TL236.B736 2007
796.7'3—dc22   2006023662

Editorial Credits
Aaron Sautter, editor; Jason Knudson, set designer; Patrick Dentinger,
   book designer; Jo Miller, photo researcher/photo editor

Photo Credits
AP/Wide World Photos/Anna Kalagani, 26
Art Directors/Darren Maybury, 12
Corbis/epa/Handout, 20–21; Jo Lillini, cover, 10–11, 24–25, 28–29; Orestis
   Panagiotou, 12–13; Sport Concept Diffusion/Jo Lillini, 19
Getty Images Inc./AFP/Damien Meyer, 18; Grazia Neri, 14–15; Luis Acosta, 27;
   Paul Kane, 4–5, 7; Reporter Images, 16–17; Ryan Pierse, 6; Tony Ashby, 8–9
Ron Kimball Stock, 22–23

1 2 3 4 5 6 12 11 10 09 08 07

TABLE OF CONTENTS

ONE WILD RIDE

A rally car charges down a dirt road. The driver spins the car sideways around a tight corner. Dirt and rocks fly everywhere.

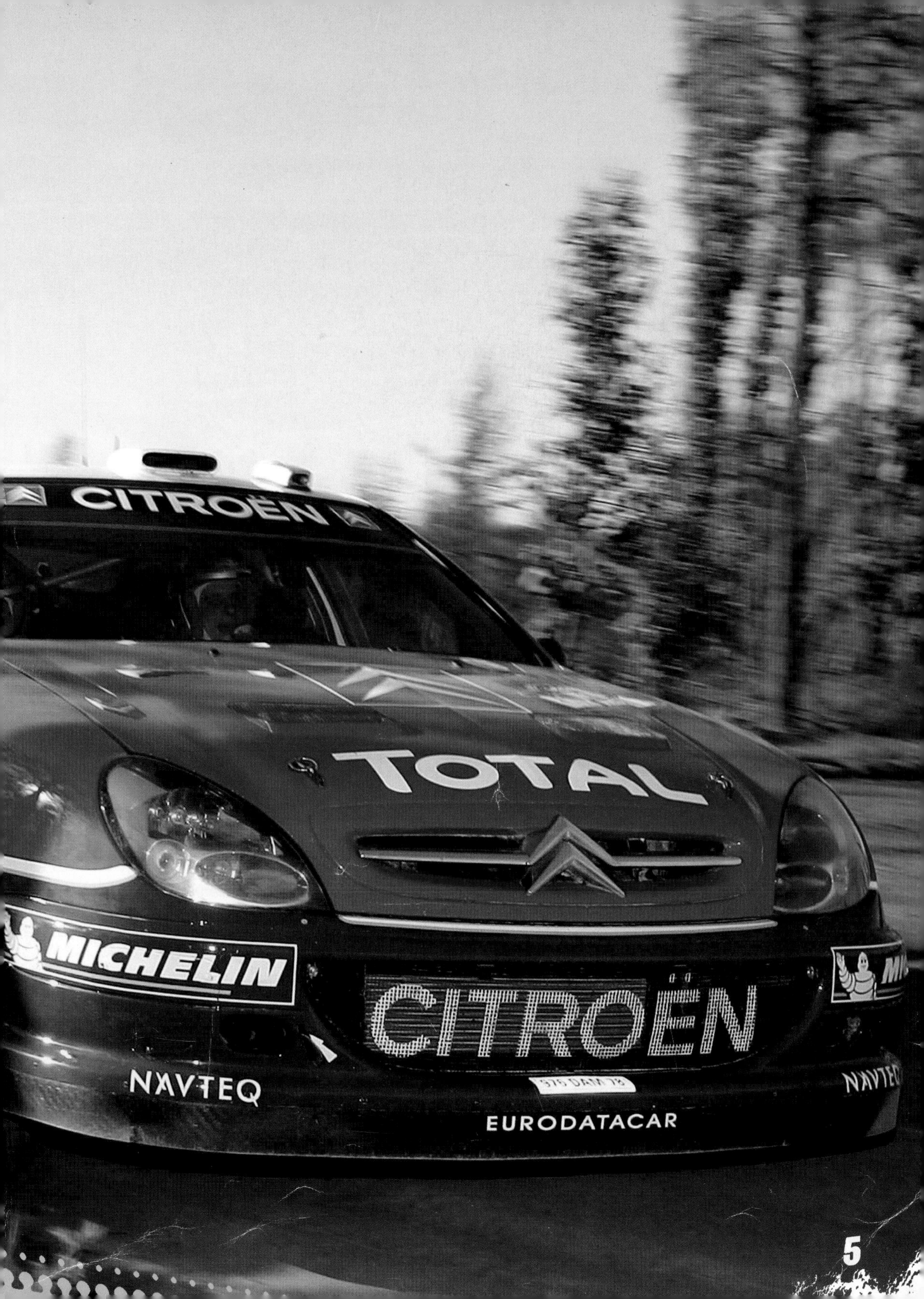
CITROËN
TOTAL
MICHELIN
CITROËN
NAVTEQ
EURODATACAR

The car surges up a hill, catches air, and lands with a thud. Suddenly, the codriver yells, "Tree!" The driver stomps on the brakes, just missing a tree.

BLAZER FACT

Codrivers are important in rally races. They give drivers directions to keep the car on the right course.

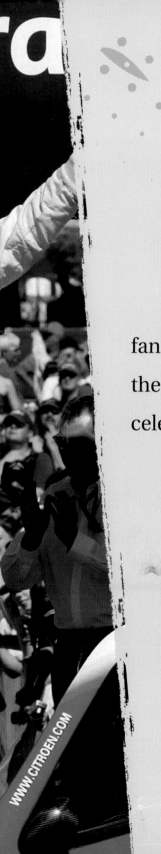

The car streaks by hundreds of fans. It crosses the finish line. It has the fastest overall time. The team celebrates its big win.

WWW.CITROEN.COM

RALLY CAR DESIGN

From a distance, rally cars look like regular cars with racing stickers. Performance updates turn rally cars into roaring race machines.

Rally cars have powerful engines. Turbochargers pump extra air and fuel into engines for more power.

BLAZER FACT

Rally fans watch the race from areas where they are safe if cars crash.

Rally car drivers push their cars to the limit. Crashes happen often. Drivers wear safety harnesses and helmets for protection. Roll cages keep car roofs from caving in.

ROUGHING IT

Rally cars start a race clean, but they finish dirty. Rally cars slosh through mud and plow through loose dirt. Even snow can't stop rally cars.

Deep-treaded tires

Rally cars need all the traction they can get. Drivers use deep-treaded tires on gravel roads. Studded tires help cars stick to icy or snowy roads.

BLAZER FACT

Strong shock absorbers and springs help rally cars go over large bumps.

Four-wheel drive gives rally cars the best grip. The engine provides power to all four wheels. The extra traction lets drivers take rally cars almost anywhere.

RALLY CAR PARTS

Air scoop

Roll cage

Air foil

Body

Deep-treaded tires

RALLY CARS IN ACTION

Pro drivers face off at many World Rally Championship (WRC) events. Dirt flies and engines roar at WRC races around the world.

The most popular rally in the world
is the Monte Carlo race in Europe. Every
year, thousands of fans flock to Monte
Carlo to cheer on their favorite team.

BLAZER FACT

Racing sections of a rally are called stages. Most rallies have 12 to 25 stages. The winning rally team has the fastest overall time.

RALLY RACING POWER!

BISHI MOTORS
RACC
Automóvil Club
pink fish
ENERGY DRINK
5717 DHS
ELIN
CALM

GLOSSARY

codriver (KO-drive-ur)—the person who gives course directions to the driver during a rally race

roll cage (ROHL KAYJ)— a structure of strong metal tubing in a rally car that keeps the roof from caving in during a crash

stud (STUD)—a small metal or rubber piece that extends from a tire to increase traction

traction (TRAK-shuhn)—the grip of a car's tires on the ground

turbocharger (TUR-boh-charj-ur)—a device that forces fuel and air into an engine to create more power

READ MORE

Beck, Paul. *Uncover a Race Car.* Uncover It. Silver Dolphin, 2003.

Savage, Jeff. *Rally Cars.* Wild Rides! Mankato, Minn.: Capstone Press, 2004.

Stille, Darlene R. *Race Cars.* Transportation. Minneapolis: Compass Point Books, 2002.

INTERNET SITES

FactHound offers a safe, fun way to find Internet sites related to this book. All of the sites on FactHound have been researched by our staff.

Here's how:
1. Visit *www.facthound.com*
2. Choose your grade level.
3. Type in this book ID **0736867848** for age-appropriate sites. You may also browse subjects by clicking on letters, or by clicking on pictures and words.
4. Click on the **Fetch It** button.

FactHound will fetch the best sites for you!

INDEX